beyond belief

beyond belief

What the Martyrs Said to God

DUANE W. H. ARNOLD
& ROBERT HUDSON

WITH AN AFTERWORD BY
MADELEINE L'ENGLE

GRAND RAPIDS, MICHIGAN 49530

ZONDERVAN™

Beyond Belief
Copyright © 2002 by Duane W. H. Arnold

The prayers in this book and the Afterword by Madeleine L'Engle were originally published in the volume by Duane W. H. Arnold *Prayers of the Martyrs* (Zondervan 1991). The introduction and biographical sketches of the martyrs are new.

Requests for information should be addressed to:

Zondervan, *Grand Rapids, Michigan 49530*

Library of Congress Cataloging-in-Publication Data

Arnold, Duane W. H.
    Beyond belief : what the martyrs said to God / Duane W. H. Arnold
        p. cm.
    ISBN 0–310–24248-7
1. Christian martyrs—Biography.   2. Christian martyrs—Prayer-books and devotions—English.   I. Hudson, Robert.   II. Title.
BR1608.5 .A76 2002
272'.092'2—dc21   2001046638

Interior design by Todd Sprague

Printed in the United States of America

---

01 02 03 04 05 06 /❖ DC/ 10 9 8 7 6 5 4 3 2 1

Contents

Introduction

It could be first-century Palestine or twenty-first century Gaza Strip. It could be a Jesuit missionary who followed the Silk Road on foot to preach the gospel to the Emperor of China or the pastor of a house church in modern Shanghai, confronting the communist state. It could be the violence of the Aztecs in the sixteenth century or the intolerance of a Latin American military junta today. It could be bearing witness to faith in Christ in a Roman court or standing before a panel of judges in Afghanistan. It could be in the distant past or it could be today—or tomorrow. It could be a first-century saint, or it could be me or you.

Late in the second century of the Christian era, a renegade charismatic theologian named Tertullian wrote that "the blood of the martyrs is the seed of the Church." He knew what it was; he saw it for himself. Certainly martyrdom was no stranger to those Christians who lived and died under the rule of a cynical and inconsistent imperial authority during the first three hundred years of the church's life. During those first centuries, countless thousands made the ultimate sacrifice of their lives as a witness to their faith in Christ. They knew what it meant to be a witness—*martyria*—literally one who showed to others by their own conduct, in their own flesh and blood, the meaning of Christ's passion in life and in death.

Yet, it is too easy to distance ourselves from the martyrs by thinking of them as historical curiosities from the early centuries of the church. In every new land where Christian missionaries have made their way, martyrs, once again, planted the seed and, all too often, nourished it with their blood. Even in so-called Christian societies—whether modern or medieval—wars of religion, disregard of conscience, and attacks upon the values of simple human dignity have called forth believers who have placed their lives on the line for the sake of Christ. When those lives have been required, they have not only been given with grace, they have been infused with grace.

That grace has often been reflected in the prayers and the writing of those who have given their lives for Christ. What they have said, what they have written, is often, quite literally, beyond belief. Collected in this small book is a sampling of prayers and reflections from these often ordinary, yet wholly remarkable people. Our selection is not exhaustive or complete, but it is suggestive of the devotion, courage, and love of those who ultimately offered their very lives in the service of Christ. Many of the selections come from actual eyewitness accounts of trials and executions; some are from the writings, set down by the martyrs themselves before the time of their death; others are taken from oral traditions later committed to writing; and a few have been located in biographies of the individuals involved. All are unique testaments of faith. The prayers are presented in contemporary language, and most have been newly translated from their original languages for inclusion in this collection. The biographies of the subjects and their prayers have been arranged chronologically for ease of access.

Most important, this book is by very nature incomplete. It cannot be complete, for day by day new pages could be added. You see, it isn't over.

It could be you.

It could be me.

It could be today.

It could be tomorrow.

Until He comes again, any of us may face that which is beyond belief.

—D.W.H.A.
August 15, 2001

beyond belief

Martyrs of
the Bible

Stephen
(died 35)

Stephen, a non-Jewish Christian living in Jerusalem, was appointed by Jesus' disciples to "wait on tables," that is, to help provide food for poor local widows. As a student of philosophy, he excelled at religious debate, and his arguments with the members of the Sanhedrin in the year 35 (recounted in Acts 7) led to his being accused of heresy by the head priests. They dragged Stephen from the city, threw him into a pit, and stoned him to death. A Pharisee named Saul was present. Later, Saul was struck by a blinding vision that led to his conversion. He has become known to history as the apostle Paul.

Stephen is considered the first of Jesus' followers to be martyred for his faith. On the day of his death, he spoke these words, recorded in Acts 7:56, 59–60:

Receive My Spirit

Look, I see heaven open
    and the Son of Man
    standing at the right hand of God....
Lord Jesus,
    receive my spirit....
Lord, do not hold this sin
    against them.

James the Just

(died 62)

Though not among the original twelve disciples, James "the Just," along with Peter, was one of the most influential leaders of the church in Jerusalem. In the letter to the church in a region called Galatia (Galatians 1:18–19), Paul even suggests that James was the chief leader, perhaps the bishop in that city. James's martyrdom is not recorded in the Bible, but early reliable sources say that he was put to death by the Sanhedrin in the year 62 by being thrown from the city walls. Echoing Jesus' own words from the cross, James spoke these words before his death:

They Are Unaware

I beg you, Lord God our Father,
Forgive them,
> for they are unaware of what
> they are doing.

Paul

(died about 65)

As a Pharisee, that is, a strict teacher of the laws of Moses, Paul worked to crush the newborn Christian faith, contributing to the deaths of many believers, including Stephen. His spectacular conversion on the road to Damascus is recorded in the book of Acts (9:1–19). As a Christian, Paul worked even more passionately to spread the gospel of Jesus than he ever did to persecute believers, and he is almost single-handedly responsible for spreading Christianity among non-Jewish people in the first century. His letters to various churches, documented in the New Testament, helped to establish the church worldwide.

The book of Acts records that Paul was imprisoned in Rome for two years. He was probably also martyred there, during the persecution of the Emperor Nero. Earlier, Paul had written to the believers in Rome these thoughts on life and death (Romans 8:35–39):

Neither Death nor Life

Who shall separate us from the love of Christ?
Shall trouble or hardship or persecution
    or famine or nakedness or danger or sword?
As it is written: "For your sake we face death all day long;
    we are considered as sheep to be slaughtered."

No, in all these things we are more than
  conquerors,
      through him who loved us.
For I am convinced that neither death nor life,
      neither angels nor demons,
      neither the present nor the future,
      nor any powers,
      neither height nor depth,
      nor anything else in all creation,
will be able to separate us from the love of God
      that is in Christ Jesus our Lord.

Later in his life, Paul wrote these words to his friend and coworker
Timothy, concerning his impending martyrdom (2 Timothy 4:6–8, 17–
18, paraphrase):

Prayer from Prison

The hour for my departure is upon me.
I have run the race,
      I have finished my course,
      I have kept the faith.
Now, the prize awaits me,
      the crown of righteousness,

Which the Lord, the righteous judge,
    will award me on that day;
And not me only, but all who love his appearing....
I was rescued out of the lion's jaws.
The Lord will rescue me
    from all evil,
    and take me safely
    into his heavenly kingdom.
To him be glory forever
    and ever! Amen.

Martyrs of the Early Church

Clement of Rome

(about 30 – about 100)

ittle is known about Clement, a Christian living in Rome, except that in the year 95 he wrote a letter to fellow believers in the Greek city of Corinth, advising them to respect their leaders and strive for harmony. This letter is important not just for its wisdom but also for its historical value, as it is probably older than some of the books of the New Testament.

Clement may have once been a slave to a cousin of the Roman Emperor Domitian and is said to have been baptized by the apostle Peter himself. Clement is thought to have become the third bishop of Rome (from 88 to 97), after Peter and a man named Cletus. It was during this time that he wrote his famous letter to the Corinthians, in which he wrote of Peter and Paul and their deaths as martyrs, concluding: "Associated with these great men of holy life is a great multitude of believers, suffering many tortures because of jealousy, some of them women who, though weak in body, completed the race of faith." Although no details of Clement's death are known, he is believed to have been martyred. He wrote:

The Sheep of Your Pasture

Lord, we beseech you to help and defend us.
Deliver the oppressed, pity the poor,
uplift those who have fallen,
be the portion of those in need,
return to your care those who have gone astray,

feed the hungry, strengthen the weak,
and break the chains of the prisoners.
May all people come to know that you only are God,
that Jesus Christ is your child,
and that we are your people and
the sheep of your pasture.

Grounded and Settled

Almighty God, Father of our Lord Jesus Christ,
grant, we pray, that we might be grounded
and settled in your truth by the coming
of your Holy Spirit into our hearts.
What we do not know,
reveal to us;
What is lacking within us,
make complete;
That which we do know,
confirm in us;
And keep us blameless in your service,
through Jesus Christ our Lord.

Direct Our Steps

Lord, by your own hand you brought to light the eternal
    fabric of the universe and created the world of humankind.
From generation to generation you are faithful, right in your
    judgments, glorious in majesty and might.
You have created and established all that exists
    in wisdom and prudence.
To look about us is to see your goodness;
    To trust in you is to know your loving kindness.
O merciful and pitying Lord, cleanse us from our sins
    and offenses, from our errors and failures.
Do not account every sin to your servants and handmaidens,
    but cleanse us by the power of your truth.
Direct our steps until we walk in purity of heart
    and our works are pleasing in your eye and in the sight
    of those who are our rulers.
Lord, show forth the light of your face upon us in peace
    for our help;
Shelter us by your mighty hand and save us from doing wrong
    by stretching forth your arm.
Deliver us from those who hate us without a cause;
To us and to all humankind grant peace and concord, even as you
    did to those who came before us when they called upon you
    truthfully and faithfully;
And cause us to be obedient both to your own almighty and
    glorious name, and to all who bear rule over us on earth.

Ignatius of Antioch
(late first to early second century)

After his arrest during a persecution of Christians in Antioch, a town in Syria, Ignatius, the local bishop, was taken to Rome for execution. On the long journey he wrote many letters to churches in Asia Minor in which he reflected on the nature of the Christian life and on the certainty of his own martyrdom. Several of these reflections follow. Most likely, he was killed, as were many other Christians, by wild beasts in the Roman arena during the time of the Emperor Trajan.

A Stream Flows

My desires are crucified,
    the warmth of my body is gone.
A stream flows,
    whispering inside me;
Deep within me it says:
    Come to the Father.

A True and Faithful Witness

Blessed be the God and Father
    of our Lord Jesus Christ,
Who of his great and abundant goodness
    willed that I should be a partaker
of the sufferings of his Christ
    and a true and faithful witness
of his divinity.

You Have Bound Me

I thank you, Lord and Master,
    that you have deemed to honor me
by making complete my love for you
    in that you have bound me with chains
of iron like those of your apostle Paul.

That I May Attain

I know what must be done. . . .
May nothing of powers visible or invisible
    prevent me,
that I may attain Jesus Christ.

Come fire and cross and grapplings
    with wild beasts,
the rending of my bones and body,
    come all the torments of the wicked one upon me.
Only let it be mine to attain Jesus Christ.

In Company with God

Near to the sword,
    I am near to God;
In the company of wild beasts,
    I am in company with God.
Only let all that happens be
    in the name of Jesus Christ,
      so that we may suffer with him.
I can endure all things if he enables me.

At Last

Now at last I am beginning
    to be a disciple.
No earthly pleasure can
    bring me any good,
    no kingdom of this world.
It is better for me to perish
    and obtain Jesus Christ
    than to rule over
    the ends of the earth.
Let me win through to the Light;
    that done, I shall be complete.
Let me suffer as my Lord suffered.

I Am God's Wheat

I am God's wheat.
May I be ground by
    the teeth of the wild beasts,
Until I become
    the fine white bread
That belongs to Christ.

Sharbil of Edessa

What a surprise it must have been for pagan worshipers of the city of Edessa when Sharbil, their high priest, converted to Christianity, especially since the Roman Emperor Trajan was savagely persecuting Christians. Sharbil, after repenting of his former life, was arrested along with his sister, Barbea, and they were ordered to renounce their newfound faith. When they refused, they were tortured with red-hot irons.

In the following prayer, spoken shortly before his death, Sharbil asks God's forgiveness for his pagan life.

The Eleventh Hour

Christ, forgive me for all of the sins I have
    committed against you,
    and all the times I provoked your anger
    by offering sacrifices to dead idols;
Have pity on me and save me.
Deliver me from the judgment to come.
Be merciful to me, as you were merciful
    to the penitent thief.
Receive me, like those who have turned to you,
    as you have turned to them.
I have entered your vineyard at the eleventh hour,
    deliver me from judgment.
Let your death, which was for the sake of sinners,
    restore me to life again the day of your coming.

Polycarp of Smyrna

(about 69 – 155)

Polycarp, born around 69, was a bishop in the city of Smyrna. Two things set him apart: first, he probably knew some of Jesus' original disciples. Second, of all the early Christian martyrs, Polycarp was one of the oldest. At the age of eighty-six, he was arrested during a pagan festival. When the authorities ordered him to renounce his faith, Polycarp replied: "For eighty-six years I have been God's servant, and he has done me no wrong. So how then can I blaspheme my King who saved me?" Enraged, his persecutors burned him to death. These prayers, written by Polycarp, show how deep his faith really was.

That Our Fruit May Abound

May God the Father,
    and the ever-living high priest Jesus Christ,
strengthen us in faith, truth, and love;
    and give to us our portion among the saints
    with all those who trust in our Lord Jesus Christ.
We pray for all saints, for kings and governors,
    for the enemies of the cross of Christ
    and for ourselves;
We pray that our fruit may abound
    and that we might be made complete in Christ Jesus our Lord.

Lord God Almighty,
Father of your beloved and blessed Child Jesus Christ,
    through whom we have come to have full knowledge of you—
God of angels and power and of all creation,
    and of all the family of the just who live before you:
I bless you that you have thought worthy this day and this hour,
    that I may be able to share in the number of the martyrs,
    to drink from the cup of your Christ,
    that I may rise and live forever, body and soul,
    in the incorruption of the Holy Spirit.
May I be admitted with those martyrs to your presence this day,
    as a welcomed and acceptable sacrifice.
You have made my life a preparation for this;
    you let me see that this was to happen,
    and now you have brought it to pass,
    for you are the true and faithful God.
For this and for all things, I praise you and give you glory,
    through the ever-living high priest,
Jesus Christ the heavenly, your dear Son.
He is with you and the Holy Spirit.
Through him may you receive glory now and forever.

Amen.

Justin Martyr
(about 100–about 165)

Justin, called "the Martyr," was a teacher and author whose special interest was the Greek philosophers Pythagoras and Plato. Though an unbeliever, Justin was an earnest seeker of truth. A chance encounter by the sea with an old Christian man, however, led Justin to a new faith, and at the age of thirty, he became a Christian. The stories of the martyrs were particularly important in his conversion; he wrote: "As a vine is pruned and trimmed, it sends forth new shoots and more abundant fruit. So it is with us Christians."

Justin traveled widely, teaching philosophy from a Christian perspective. While in Rome, he is said to have presented one of his books to the Emperor Marcus Aurelius, himself a lover of philosophy. Justin carried on a heated debate with a local philosopher named Crescens, a man who may have been responsible for having Justin arrested. The trial transcripts still exist. When asked to sacrifice to the Roman gods, Justin stated, "No man in his right mind willingly exchanges truth for falsehood." The local prefect sentenced Justin to beheading, at which point Justin made this simple but moving statement of his faith:

I Ask Nothing More

I ask nothing more than to suffer
> for the cause of my Lord Jesus Christ
> and by this, to be saved.

31

If I can do this,

> then I can stand in confidence and quiet
> before the judgment seat of my God and Savior,
> when, in accordance with his will,
> this world passes away.

Apollonius the Apologist

(died about 185)

During the reign of the Roman Emperor Commodius, Christians were tolerated because the emperor's wife was sympathetic to them and may have even become a Christian herself. But Christians were expected to keep their faith strictly private, since the anti-Christian laws of the previous emperor, Marcus Aurelius, were still in effect.

Apollonius was a prominent senator in Rome. Moved by reading Christian writers, he secretly converted. One of his servants, however, betrayed him to the local prefect, a man named Perennis, who, by the way, also had that same slave executed as an informer. Apollonius passionately defended his faith before Perennis, a defense that earned Apollonius the nickname "the Apologist." When Perennis asked him, "So, do you *want* to die?" Apollonius made the following famous response. It did not help his cause, for the prefect found him guilty nonetheless and sentenced him to having his legs crushed and then to be beheaded.

Nothing Greater

I enjoy life;
    but love of life has not
    made me afraid to die.
There is nothing greater than life—
    that eternal life that gives
    immortality to the soul of the righteous.

Little is known about the man named Shamuna and his friend Guria except that they came from the city of Edessa and were martyred sometime late in the second century. They were apparently poor, elderly working men, who were arrested for no other reason than being Christians. After a lengthy interrogation by the local governor, they were tortured, hung upside down by their feet, and then beheaded. The following prayer is attributed to Shamuna just before his death.

The Conflict Closed

You are God of all,
>   and to you belongs glory and praise,
because it has pleased you that we should
>   carry on to its close the conflict that we have entered,
>   and that we should receive at your hands
>   the brightness that shall never fade away.
God and Father of our Lord Jesus Christ,
>   in peace receive our spirits to yourself.

(about 170 – 236)

We tend to think of early Christians as a tightly knit band of believers bravely facing Roman persecution. They often, however, fought among themselves when they felt that essential religious issues were at stake. Hippolytus, born around 170, was a bishop in Rome and a controversial writer and thinker. At one point, he so strongly disagreed with the Bishop of Rome that he set himself up as an alternative bishop. As events unfolded, however, Hippolytus was exiled to the island of Sardinia along with Pontianus, a successor to the bishop that Hippolytus had denounced.

Hippolytus's greatness lies not so much in his powerful writings or his martyrdom. In fact, we are not sure he was actually martyred, though one source suggests he may have been torn apart by horses. His greatness, rather, lies in the fact that he reconciled himself to his religious enemies before his death. Hippolytus wrote the following joyful resurrection hymn.

Christ Is Risen!

Christ is risen:
> The world below lies desolate.

Christ is risen:
> The spirits of evil are fallen.

Christ is risen:
> The angels of God are rejoicing.

Christ is risen:

    The tombs of the dead are empty.

Christ is risen indeed from the dead,

    The first of the sleepers.

Glory and power are his forever and ever.

                                Amen.

Carpus of Gurdos

(died about 250)

The authenticity of early Christian martyr stories is often uncertain. The story of Carpus, however, is taken from a history book based on real Roman court records, so the details are reliable. Carpus was a bishop in the town of Gurdos in Asia Minor. With several other people he was arrested as a Christian and tried by Valerius, the Roman governor in the city of Pergamos. Carpus and his friends were cross-examined three times and ordered to sacrifice to the Roman gods. When they refused, one of their companions was whipped to death in their presence. When the remaining Christians were again ordered to renounce their faith and sacrifice to the gods, Carpus responded:

I Am a Christian

You ask me
    what I am.
I am a Christian.
I worship Christ,
    the Son of God, for he came
    in these last days to save us,
    and he has delivered us
    from the snares of the wicked one.
I will not sacrifice to idols.
The living do not sacrifice to the dead.

At another point in the inquisition, Carpus prayed:

Unworthy Though I May Be

I will always bless you,
    Lord Jesus Christ, Son of God,
For you have considered me
    as being fit to share your fate,
Unworthy though I may be.

Eventually, Carpus and the others were condemned to death, the most grisly death being reserved for Carpus by having his skin torn from his body. His last words were:

Blessed Are You

Blessed are you,
    Lord Jesus Christ, Son of God,
because you have judged me, a sinner,
    worthy to have a part in your suffering.

Agathonice of Pergamos
(died about 250)

gathonice, a Christian woman of Pergamos, was the sister of the deacon Papylus (see next entry) and a disciple of the bishop Carpus (see previous entry), and she was one of the believers arrested and tried along with the bishop. She prayed these two prayers, which are recorded in the trial transcripts, moments before her execution.

Shelter

My God, shelter my children,
    for I am being taken from them.
Help me, Lord Jesus,
    since I bear this suffering for you.

Come to Help Me

Lord, Lord, Lord,
    please come to help me;
I turn to you alone
    for my refuge.

Papylus, a deacon, was arrested along with his sister, Agathonice, and their bishop, Carpus (see the previous two entries). He was the last of the three to be interrogated. With all of Papylus's companions dead, the Roman governor Valerius hoped that Papylus might renounce his faith. Papylus still refused and was tortured. After enduring his tortures silently for a long time, Papylus said: "I feel no pain because someone comforts me—someone you can't see because he suffers inside me." The governor then ordered him to be killed. These are the last, simple words that Papylus spoke.

Benediction

Blessed are you, Lord Jesus Christ,
    Son of God,
for you have, in your mercy,
    been so kind
as to allow me a death like yours.

Agatha of Catania

(died about 250)

Aside from the fact that she was born in Sicily, much of our information about the martyr named Agatha is based on legend. The most common story is that she was the beautiful daughter of a wealthy family and that she secretly became a Christian. When a local Roman consul named Quintian tried to force her to marry him, she refused, vowing to spend her life as a virgin. In his fury, Quintian had her imprisoned in a house of prostitution, where she continued to cling to her virginity and her faith. Frustrated, Quintian had her brought to trial on charges of being a Christian. In prison she was tortured by having her body mutilated, after which she was denied all medicine, bandages, and food. She died in prison from her injuries. The following prayer is attributed to her.

Receive Now My Soul

O Lord, my creator, from my birth
    you have always protected me;
You have taken from me the love of the world
    and given me patience to suffer.
Receive now my soul.

Nestor of Magydus
(died 251)

Many early Christians were persecuted for political rather than religious reasons. Epolius, the governor of Lycia, Pamphylia, and Phrygia, thought he could win the favor of the Roman Emperor Decius by initiating a general persecution of Christians. The governor chose Nestor, a local bishop in the town of Magydus, as his victim because of Nestor's outspoken evangelism. Nestor was arrested, ordered to sacrifice to the Roman gods, and when he refused—which Epolius fully expected—he was crucified. Early records attribute this simple prayer to Nestor:

With My Christ

With my Christ I have ever been,
With my Christ I am now,
With my Christ I will be forever;
  you only will I confess.

ittle is known of Nemesian, a bishop who lived near Numidia in the early third century. He was arrested in 257 during the persecutions instigated by the Roman emperor Valerian. Along with nine other local bishops, ministers, and members of their various churches, he was sentenced to hard labor in the marble quarries of Sigum. All of them died from the privation and hardship they experienced. These words of encouragement were spoken by Nemesian to his friends as they labored in the quarries:

A Bidding Prayer

Let us help each other
    by our prayers,
so that God and Christ
    and the whole choir of angels
may come to our aid
    in our time of suffering,
when we shall need their
    assistance the most.

Cyprian of Carthage
(died 258)

At midlife, Cyprian, a native of Carthage in North Africa, had it all. He was a respected writer, speaker, and political leader—wealthy and comfortable. But about 246, he became friends with an elderly priest, Caecilianus, and converted to Christianity. When the old priest died, Cyprian sold all his own possessions to care for the deceased man's family.

Two years later, about 248, he became bishop of Carthage, although he left in 249 to escape persecutions. After returning to Carthage again six years later, he was caught up in a new wave of persecutions, arrested, and put on trial. When he refused to sacrifice to the pagan gods, he was beheaded on September 14, 258. He is said to have paid the executioner twenty-five gold coins from his own pocket. These prayers, the first for his persecutors and the second for the church in general, are from his writings.

May Their Rage Subside

We pray that the God whom the enemies
    of the church are always provoking
    would tame their unruly hearts.
May their rage subside and peace
    return to their hearts;
May their minds, clouded by sin,
    turn and see the light;
May they seek the prayers of the bishop
    and not his blood.

Prayer for the Church

Good God, may we confess your name to the end;
May we emerge unmarked and glorious
   from the traps and darkness of this world.
As you have bound us together
   by charity and peace,
And as together we have persevered
   under persecution,
So may we also rejoice together
   in your heavenly kingdom.

Montanus and His Friends

(died 258)

ontanus, Flavian, and six other priests and deacons were disciples of the North African bishop Cyprian (see previous entry). A year after Cyprian's death, the local Roman governor managed to throw Montanus and the others into prison on trumped-up charges. The eight men were given almost no food or water for several months before their executions. Since the Emperor Valerian decreed that only "bishops, priests, and deacons" should be killed, some of Flavian's friends tried to have him released by claiming that he was not a deacon. But Flavian, ashamed of their dishonesty, confessed to the governor that he was indeed a deacon. When Montanus, Flavian's friend, was led to the ax-man's block, Montanus tore his own blindfold in half, declaring that the other half was for Flavian, who was, in fact, martyred three days later. The following prayer was written by either Montanus or one of his friends while in prison.

The Bond of Love

We all have the same spirit,
    and this is what unites us in our actions
    and all that we do together.
This is the bond of love that puts evil to flight
    and that which is most pleasing to God;

It is by our praying together that we receive
    what we ask.
These are the ties that link our hearts together,
    and make mere mortals the children of God.
To inherit your kingdom, O God,
    we must be your children;
To be your children,
    we must love one another.

Genesius of Rome Genesius of Rome
Genesius of Rome Genesius of Rome
Genesius of Rome Genesius of Rome

Genesius of Rome

(died about 286)

Movie actors often "thank God" when accepting an Academy Award—as though acknowledging their faith publicly were an act of courage. But imagine an actor being willing to die for such a statement.

It is impossible to disentangle fact and legend in the story of the Roman actor Genesius. The story says he was the leading actor in a Roman theater company that, at the time, was performing before the Emperor Diocletian himself. The play was a profane parody of the then-illegal Christian sect, but when Genesius enacted a mock baptism, he felt an inexplicable presence take hold of him, and he was, according to legend, converted. When he announced to the emperor and audience that he was now a Christian, it was at first taken as a joke. But when he persisted, he aroused the emperor's anger, and Diocletian ordered him tortured and beheaded. Genesius is thought to have died around 286, or according to some sources, later. Although scholars doubt its authenticity, a seventh-century account attributes the following prayer to Genesius, the actor whose role became a reality.

Christ Is in My Heart

There is but one king that I know:
It is he whom I love and worship.
If I were to be killed a thousand times
    for my loyalty to him,
    I would still be his servant.
Christ is on my lips,
Christ is in my heart;
    no amount of suffering will take him from me.

48

Donatian of Nantes

Two brothers, Rogatian, the older, and Donatian, lived in the town of Nantes, in Roman France (then called Gaul). Upon his conversion, Donation began to be an outspoken evangelist, but because his zeal drew the attention of the authorities, he was arrested. Inspired by his brother's faith, Rogatian too became a Christian, but since the local bishop had been arrested earlier, Rogatian could find no one to baptize him. After Rogatian was also arrested, the two brothers suffered martyrdom together by having their heads pierced with lances and then being beheaded. The night before their martyrdom, however, Donatian spoke the following prayer on behalf of his as-yet-unbaptized brother, Rogatian.

Simple Faith

Lord Jesus Christ, when the desire is from the heart,
    you account it as the deed.
When the hindrance to its reality is only the inability
    to carry out the deed,
    we know that the intention alone is sufficient.
Although you have given us the power
    to choose what we might wish to do,
    the power to bring that choice to reality is yours alone.

May the simple faith of your servant Rogatian
    [although he is unbaptized] be accounted
    as though it were the gift of baptism;
And if tomorrow the governor is insistent
    and puts us to the sword,
May the shedding of your servant's blood be for him
    as though it were the sacrament of anointing.

Martyrs in the Time of the Emperor Diocletian

Felix of Tibiuca

(died 303)

Gaius Aurelius Valerius Diocletianus (245–313), known simply as Diocletian, was the emperor of Rome from 284 to 305. For the first part of his reign, he was largely sympathetic to the Christian religion, but through the intrigues of one of his advisers, Galerius, Diocletian initiated the last great wave of Roman persecutions against Christians. He decreed, on pain of death, that all churches should surrender their Bibles and that all Christians should sacrifice to the Roman gods. The decree stood for eight years after Diocletian's abdication in 305. Only when he died, in 313, did the persecutions end, by edict of the new emperor, and the first nominal Christian ruler of Rome, Constantine I.

Sometime near the beginning of Diocletian's persecutions, a Christian bishop named Felix, in the town of Tibiuca in North Africa, refused to turn over his church's copy of the Bible to the local Roman authorities. Along with several other believers, he was arrested and beheaded on July 15, 303. The following prayer is thought to be his.

You Are Merciful

Lord, I give you thanks.
You are merciful to grant me this release.
God, I give you thanks.
I have lived in this world for fifty-six years.
I have kept myself pure, I have followed the gospel,
> I have preached the faith,
>> and I have taught nothing but the truth.

Jesus Christ, Lord God of heaven and earth,
    I give myself to you in sacrifice,
    for you are the eternal one.
Glory and power are yours and will be forever.

Julitta of Caesarea

(died about 303)

Basil, one of the great writers of the early Christian church, tells the story of a woman named Julitta, a wealthy widow in the town of Caesarea in Cappadocia (modern-day Turkey). When one of her neighbors claimed a portion of her land as his own, she took him to court, not knowing that he had a devious plan up his sleeve. He knew that Julitta was secretly a Christian and that the Emperor Diocletian had recently decreed that Christians should sacrifice to the pagan gods. So, when Julitta won her court trial and regained her lands, the neighbor accused her before the judge as a Christian. When the judge asked her if this was true, rather than deny her faith, she confessed. Before she was taken away to be burned alive, she is said to have spoken the following words to the judge:

An Exchange

Let the estates I own be ravaged
    or given to others;
Let me lose my life,
    and let my body be destroyed;
Rather than that I should speak one word
    against the Lord, who made me.
If they take from me a small portion
    of this earth and its wealth
I shall exchange it for heaven.

Serenus the Gardener

(died about 303)

Serenus, known as "the Gardener," came from Greece and traveled to Dalmatia (modern-day Yugoslavia) to live. When the persecutions began in that region, Serenus, like many other Christians, fled and kept his faith a secret. He lived, according to legend, as a hermit and nurtured a particularly beautiful garden.

One day, a Roman officer's wife and her daughters strolled through Serenus's garden at a time of day when well-born women were not supposed to be walking about. Serenus asked her to leave and to return at an appropriate hour, but the woman took offense and brought the gardener to trial. When the local governor heard Serenus's side of the story, however, he immediately dismissed the case. But something in Serenus's manner made the governor suspect that he might be a Christian, so he asked Serenus if he would sacrifice to the Roman gods. In reply, Serenus spoke these words, which earned him a martyr's death:

A Stone Fit for Building

It has pleased the Lord
  to keep me until this time.
I thought, for a while,
  that he had rejected me as being
  a stone not fit for his building;
but now that he has called me to take my place in it,
I am ready to suffer that I may have a part
  in his kingdom with all the saints.

Afra of Augsburg

(died 304)

fra worked as a prostitute in the Roman city of Augsburg. One day, a Spanish bishop named Narcissus arrived in the town and asked Afra, whose profession he didn't know, for a place to stay. Afra agreed, and when Roman guards arrived at her house to arrest the bishop, Afra successfully hid him beneath a pile of flax. The bishop's holiness and steadfastness to his faith so attracted Afra that she renounced her profession and converted to Christianity, along with her mother, Hilaria, and several of their servants.

Soon, however, Afra was herself arrested and martyred by being tied to a tree and burned to death. When her mother built a shrine at her daughter's tomb, she too was martyred—by being burned alive in their house along with their servants. Afra is said to have spoke this simple prayer before her death:

An Offering by Fire

I thank you, Lord Jesus Christ,
    for your goodness in accepting me,
an offering by fire for your name's sake;
    for you offered yourself upon the cross
as a sacrifice for the sins
    of all the world.
I offer myself in death to you,
    who lives and reigns
with the Father and the Holy Spirit,
    ages without end.

                       Amen.

We tend to think of Roman soldiers as persecutors of Christians. If, however, the centurion in Matthew 8:5–13 is any indication, many soldiers became Christians themselves. One such person, Ferreolus, even became a noted saint. He was an army *tribune*, that is, an officer assigned to help protect ordinary people from the whims of the local Roman rulers and soldiers. One law had been established for the entire empire, and the military tribunes acted as judges when the common people felt they had been unfairly treated.

Ferreolus was stationed in the outpost town of Vienne in France. When Julian, a Christian from the nearby town of Brioud, asked Ferreolus to protect him from persecution, the tribune agreed. Whether Julian converted the tribune to Christianity or whether Ferreolus was already sympathetic to Christians is not known.

The local Roman governor, Crispin, however, found out about the fugitive and ordered the immediate arrest of both Ferreolus and Julian, who were whipped, imprisoned, and finally beheaded at the command of the governor. The first prayer is attributed to Ferreolus the tribune, and the second to Julian.

I Am Willing

Lord, I seek little of this
    world's wealth.
If I may only be allowed to live and
    serve you, I would be content.

If, however, this seems too much
    in the eyes of those who persecute me,
I am willing to give up my life
    before I forsake my faith.

Last Prayer

I have been too long
    in this world of strife;
I would be with Jesus.

Dativus the Senator

(died 304)

What if simply going to church were illegal? What if the government burned every Bible it could get its hands on? Imagine the police breaking down the door of your church one Sunday and arresting the entire congregation.

That is exactly what happened in the town of Abitine, in North Africa, to a local priest named Saturninus and fifty other men, women, and children in the year 304. In response to Diocletian's decree that all Bibles should be handed over to the authorities and burned, one bishop in Abitine, rather than face martyrdom, shamefully agreed. According to legend, a sudden rainstorm extinguished the flames of the Bible bonfire.

One of the local priests, Saturninus, flatly refused. Roman soldiers broke into their church during a Sunday worship service, arrested everyone, and marched them in heavy chains to the city of Carthage for their trial. Led by Saturninus and Dativus, a respected local senator, the group sang hymns and prayed along the entire route. Because of his prestigious position in the senate, Dativus the Senator was the first to be tried, and during the interrogation, he spoke the following prayer.

Let Me Not Be Put to Shame

Lord Christ, let me not be put to shame.
Christ, I beseech you,
    let me not be put to shame.
Christ, come to my aid,
    have pity on me,
    let me not be put to shame.
Christ, I beseech you, give me the strength
    to suffer what I must for you.

Saturninus the Younger of Abitine
(died 304)

After Dativus the Senator had been questioned and tortured (see the previous reading), Anulinus, the local proconsul asked the other believers from Abitine why they stubbornly continued to worship on Sunday despite the imperial edict. One of the prisoners replied: "It is not lawful for us to omit the duty of that day.... We will keep the commandments of God at the expense of our lives." Frustrated and angry, the proconsul condemned them to death. Saturninus, the priest's own son, prayed this prayer before his execution.

Life Beyond Death

Lord Christ, I ask only that I might have
    the strength to endure what I must.
Lord Christ, I put my trust in you
    that you will grant me life beyond death.

Thelica of Abitine

(died 304)

Among the believers tried along with the priest Saturninus and Dativus the senator (see the previous two readings) was a man named Thelica. As his friends and fellow believers suffered torture, awaited execution, or died of hunger in the harsh Roman prison, Thelica recited these prayers during those dark days:

The Eternal Kingdom

The eternal kingdom is within sight,
    a kingdom that shall suffer no loss.
Lord Jesus Christ, we are Christians,
    we are your servants;
You alone are our hope,
    the hope of all Christians.
God Almighty, God most high:
    we give you praise,
    we give praise to your name.

Thanks be to God.
O Christ, Son of God, deliver your servants
    by the power of your name.
O God most high, do not consider the actions of
    my persecutors as sin.
God, have pity on them.
Lord, for the sake of your name,
    grant me the strength to endure what I must.
Release your servants from the captivity of this world.
My God, I thank you,
    though I cannot thank you as I should.

Emeritus of Abitine

(died 304)

Another of the fifty-one believers of Abitine who were tortured and condemned to death by Anulinus, the Roman proconsul (see the previous readings), was a man named Emeritus. The early records of the trial say that he spoke this prayer before his execution.

Accept My Praise

O Christ, I implore you,
    accept my praise.
Christ, deliver me:
It is for you that I suffer.
Lord Christ, the time of trial is short,
    I will endure it with joy.

We sometimes picture Christian martyrs as impoverished believers huddled in dank catacombs. Crispina, however, was born into a rich family in the town of Thagara in North Africa. She married a prominent businessman and had several children.

After being arrested as a Christian, she was put on trial by the local proconsul, Anulinus (the same man who executed the fifty-one believers from Abitine, see previous readings), and ordered to sacrifice to the Roman gods. When she refused, declaring that she honored "only one God," she was sentenced to having her head shaved and her body "exposed"—that is, she was chained naked in the public square so that passersby could mock her. She remained faithful to God throughout her ordeal, however, and it is said that not even the tears of her children could persuade her to give up her faith. Finally, she was condemned to beheading in the town of Thebeste in Numidia on December 5, 304. This prayer is reliably thought to have been spoken by Crispina herself, as recorded in a book written not long after her death.

Strengthen My Soul

O God, who was and is,
    you willed that I should be born.
You brought me to salvation
    through the waters of baptism.
Be with me now and strengthen my soul
    that I will not weaken.
Praise to God who has looked upon me
    and delivered me from my enemies.

Severus of Thrace

(died 304)

Severus was a deacon in the church of Heraclea, near Constantinople, under the leadership of the local bishop, an aged man named Philip (see the following entry). These men, along with two priests, Eusebius and Hermes, were arrested for their faith. When the authorities closed their church, Philip said to the soldiers: "Do you think God lives within these walls? No, he lives in the hearts of his people." During their trial, the four men agreed to hand over the church's various possessions, but when they refused to give up their Bible, they were whipped and ordered to sacrifice to Hercules, the local deity of the city of Heraclea. Again they refused. The men were then confined to prison for seven months. After another short trial, they were sentenced to death by fire. The following prayer was written by Severus while in prison, awaiting execution.

Allow Me to Share

To those who are tried by the tempest, you are the calm harbor;
    you are the object of all that hope.
To those who are sick, you are health;
    you guide the blind and give help to those in need.
To those who face suffering, you always grant mercy,
    you are a light in darkness, a place of rest for the weary.

You brought forth the land, you rule the sea,
     all creation is set in its place by you;
By your word the heavens and the stars
     were created and made complete.
Noah was kept safe and Abraham given increase by you.
Isaac was released and a sacrifice was provided by you.
Jacob found sweet confusion as he struggled with you.
Lot was delivered from the judgment of Sodom by you.
You allowed Moses to see you, and you gave wisdom to Joshua.
Your mercy attended Joseph in exile,
     and you brought your people out of the land of Egypt.
You led your people into the land that you had promised them.
The three children in the furnace were protected by you,
     they were covered by your dew
     and the flames could not do them any harm.
Daniel was sustained and given life, for you closed the mouths
     of the lions.
Jonah was not allowed to die in the sea,
     for when the leviathan caught him,
     you allowed him to escape unharmed.
Judith was given the weapons she required.
Susanna was delivered from the unjust judges by you.
You gave Esther her triumph; you cast down Aman.
You have delivered us from darkness into light eternal,
     your unquenchable light.

Father of our Lord and Savior Jesus Christ:
You gave to me the sign of the cross—the sign of Christ.
I ask you, Lord, do not count me unworthy of the suffering
that has been endured by my brothers.
Allow me to share the crown with them.
Allow us to be together in glory
as we have been together in prison.
Allow me to find my rest with them,
as we have confessed your glorious name together.

Philip was the elderly bishop of Heraclea, a region in the country of Thrace, not far from Constantinople. He was arrested along with the deacon Severus (see previous entry) and two priests, Hermes and Eusebius. After his interrogation by the judge, Philip was dragged by the feet back to his cell, and he was so badly injured that he had to be carried to the stake to be burned to death. This is his last prayer before dying:

You Have Called Me

Lord, you have shown me
    what I must suffer.
As a dove descending,
    offering me food that is sweet,
So I know that you have called me
    and honored me with a martyr's death.

(died 304)

Andronicus was from a wealthy family in Pompeiopolis, Cilicia. He was arrested as a Christian along with two other Christians, Probus and Tarachus, and together they were cross-examined by the local governor, Numerian Maximus. Since the men remained steadfast in their faith, they were tortured and then placed, gravely wounded, in the arena. When the starving, wild animals released to torment them took little interest in their prey, gladiators were dispatched to kill them with swords.

What is remarkable about these three men is that the text of their interrogation still exists, thought to be taken from the actual Roman records. At one point during Andronicus's interrogation, the governor ordered that his wounds be rubbed with salt, but the torturer replied that the wounds had already closed so that salt could not be applied. When the governor expressed his amazement, Andronicus said, simply:

He Heals by His Word

The physician our Savior
    is all powerful.
He restores those who worship
    the Lord and hope in him.
He heals not by men's cunning,
    but by his word.
Though he dwells in heaven,
    he is present everywhere.
All praise to him.

Theodotus of Ancyra

(died 304)

That there was a martyr named Theodotus in the city of Ancyra in Asia Minor is fairly certain, but legend has clouded the facts. According to the romantic but probably fictional story, Theodotus was an innkeeper, a Christian, who helped hide many persecuted Christians. Whenever possible, he would recover the bodies of the dead to give them proper burial. It was on one such errand of mercy—while recovering the bodies of seven women who had been tied to stones and thrown into a lake—that he himself was betrayed by his own brother, taken prisoner, and eventually executed. Earlier, when a local priest had said that the region needed a great martyr to galvanize the local Christians into a strong fellowship, Theodotus had told him that he wished he could be just such a martyr. The following prayer is attributed to Theodotus, the innkeeper of Ancyra.

Grant Peace to Your Church

Lord Jesus Christ, creator of heaven and earth;
>   you will never abandon those who put their trust in you.
We give you thanks:
>   you have prepared us to live in your heavenly city
>   and share in your kingdom.
We give you thanks:
>   you have strengthened us to overcome the serpent
>   and crush its head.
Grant rest to your servants,
>   let the violence of their enemies be placed upon me.
Grant peace to your Church:
>   may it be delivered from the oppression of the Wicked One.

Januarius of Cordova

(died about 304)

The range of Diocletian's persecution was immense. From the far reaches of Turkey to the southern tip of Spain, Christians lost their lives. In about 304, a man named Januarius and two of his friends, Faustus and Martial, were arrested in the city of Cordova, Spain—simply for being Christians. They were tortured by having their faces disfigured and then they were burned alive. The Christian poet Prudentius later referred to them as the "Three Crowns of Cordova." This prayer is attributed to Januarius.

My Comfort

Jesus Christ is my comfort.
It is you who created us all.
There is only you, one God,
 Father, Son, and Holy Spirit,
  to whom homage and praise are due.

Irenaeus of Sirmium

(died 304)

An early biography exists of a bishop named Irenaeus and is considered reliable. He lived in the city of Pannonia (in the former Yugoslavia). Like so many others, Irenaeus was interrogated by the local Roman governor, a man named Probus, for his refusal to sacrifice to the Roman gods. But Probus hit upon an unusual idea. He ordered all the bishop's family to witness his torture and informed them that Irenaeus would be put to death if they failed to convince him to renounce his faith. In spite of his children and wife's desperate pleading, Irenaeus steadfastly replied with the words of Jesus: "If anyone renounces me before men, I will renounce him before the Father in heaven." He was then taken to a bridge, beheaded, and his body thrown into the river. According to the biography, these were his final words:

Take Me to Yourself

I give you thanks, Lord Jesus Christ:
In the midst of my trials and suffering
    you have granted me the strength not to waver;
By your mercy, you have given me a share of glory eternal.
Lord Jesus Christ, your compassion caused you to suffer
    to save the world.

May the heavens open and the angels receive my spirit,
    for I am suffering for you and your church in this place.
I beseech you, merciful Lord, please take me to yourself
    and strengthen the faith of your servants who remain.

Euplius the Deacon

(died 304)

We seldom think of owning a Bible as something rare—or dangerous. But historically, since the time of Jesus, most people have been unable to either read or write, depending upon priests and ministers to read the Bible to them. Since copies were expensive, even Christians who could read rarely owned their own Bibles.

Euplius was a deacon in the town of Catania, on the island of Sicily. In 304, when the soldiers of the local Roman governor, Calvisian, discovered that Euplius actually owned a copy of the Gospels, the governor ordered him to burn the book as a sacrifice to the Roman gods; Euplius refused. In prison, Euplius stoutly continued to refuse to go against his faith, and as a result, he was beheaded on April 29, 304. Here is one of Euplius's final prayers. He was a man who knew the strength God gives to people through his Word.

For This, O Christ, I Thank You

For this, O Christ, I thank you.
Keep me in your care,
    for I am suffering, owing to my faith in you.
I worship the Father, the Son, and the Holy Spirit.
I worship the Holy Trinity,
    apart from you there is no other God.

For this, O Christ, I thank you.
Lord, the glory you receive from those whom you
    in your mercy have summoned, is great.
Lord, protect all of your servants:
    remain with them until the end,
    for then they will glorify your name for all eternity.
For this, Lord Jesus Christ, I give you thanks:
    your strength has sustained me;
You have kept my soul from perishing;
    you have granted to me grace, the grace of your name.
Now complete that which has been begun in me
    and by this put the Adversary to shame.

Pteleme the Copt

(died about 304)

Pteleme the Copt was a martyr of the church in Egypt. According to tradition, he was blinded by the Roman authorities before being beheaded, sometime in the early years of the fourth century.

Until My Enemies Know

God, hear me when I cry to you;
My Lord Jesus, do not forsake me,
      but come to me quickly;
For there is no God apart from you,
      be with me until my enemies know
      that you alone are God;
For yours is the power and the glory,
      forever and ever.

                              Amen.

Shenoufe the Copt

(died about 304)

According to Coptic tradition preserved in the Pierpont Morgan codices, Shenoufe was arrested during the general persecution started by the Emperor Diocletian, along with eleven other members of his family. The entire family is said to have died under torture. Here are three of Shenoufe's prayers:

I Bless You, Jesus

I bless you, Jesus,
  to you belong all blessings.
I bless you, Jesus,
  you are the only begotten of the Father.
I bless you, Jesus,
  you are the true vine,
  the crown upon the throne of the Father.
I bless you, Jesus,
  you walked upon the water,
  and your feet remained dry.
I bless you, Jesus,
  you made the bitter waters sweet.
I bless you, Jesus,
  you are the staff held by the Father.

79

I bless you, Jesus,
    you are the unmovable rock.
I bless you, Jesus,
    you command the angels.
I bless you, Jesus,
    and your good Father, in whose hands
    is our breath, and who gives us life.
For yours is the power and the glory, forever.
                                        Amen.

Hear Us, O God

Hear us, O God, the Father of our Lord Jesus Christ.
Through your name the sea is calmed,
    the fire is quenched and the grave
    and death are brought to nothing.
You comfort those who are oppressed,
    you heal those who are suffering;
Those who are lost in the sea,
    you come to their aid;
In like manner, my Lord, also come
    to help us and deliver us from this time;
For you are the true God,
    the help of those who are oppressed
    and in tribulation,
    and yours is the power and the glory forever.
                                        Amen.

You Have Heard Us

You have heard us,
    O king of those in heaven and earth;
You have not allowed us to be
    put to shame;
But you have brought us and all
    who hear you to glory;
For you alone are God in heaven and earth
    with your beloved son, Jesus Christ.

Sophia of Alexandria

(died about 304)

Sophia was a Coptic woman, the sister of Shenoufe (see previous entry). She was one of the eleven family members arrested along with her brother. Here is a prayer spoken by her and written in the early records:

The Crown

My Lord Jesus Christ,
Even as you have heard my brethren entreating you,
    and have accepted their sacrifice,
Even so, hear me when I cry to you;
May I also be counted worthy of the victor's crown
    which they have received.

Paese the Copt

(died about 304)

Little is known about the man Paese, a Coptic Christian of the early fourth century, except that he was an Egyptian and the brother of a woman named Thecla. Together they were arrested and executed under the persecutions of the Emperor Diocletian. Their memory, as well as the following powerful prayer, spoken by Paese, are preserved in certain ancient writings of the Coptic church.

You Gave Strength

Lord God Almighty,
    the Father of our Lord Jesus Christ,
You gave strength to your prophets
    and your holy apostles,
You gave strength to your holy martyrs,
May you also give strength to us,
    and protect us from harm.
Take our souls to yourself with our
    faces unashamed.
To you be glory, and to your beloved
    and holy Son, Jesus Christ,
        and the Holy Spirit, forever and ever.
                    Amen.

(died 308)

Quirinus was a bishop in the city of Siscia, in what is now called Croatia. About 308, Galerius, one of the local Roman authorities, was actively persecuting the Christians in the region. Like many of the early Christians, Quirinus believed that it was better to flee persecution in order to continue preaching the gospel, than to offer oneself up willingly for death. So Quirinus fled. Like many other Christians, however, Quirinus did not refuse martyrdom when it became unavoidable. He was captured by the authorities, brought back to Siscia, and ordered to sacrifice to the Roman gods. When he refused, he was beaten and sent to the regional governor in a city called Sabaria (now in Hungary). When he again refused to renounce his faith, his sentence was to have a millstone tied around his neck and be thrown into the Raab River. The following prayer is attributed to him:

I Will Worship

God, you are with me
    and you can help me;
You were with me when I was taken,
    and you are with me now.
You strengthen me.

The God I serve is everywhere—
    in heaven and earth and the sea,
but he is above them all,
    for all live in him:
All were created by him,
    and by him only do they remain.
I will worship only the true God;
    you will I carry in my heart;
No one on earth shall be able to
    separate me from you.

(died 311)

little is known about Methodius, except that he was a bishop in the town of Olympus in Lycia, Asia Minor (modern-day Greece), who wrote many poems and treatises. Two of his treatises were entitled *On the Resurrection* and *The Symposium*, but all of his writings, except the following prayer, have been lost.

Beyond the Gates of Life

Blessed Father, eternal,
    binding all creation together
    by your strength,
Taking the heavens for your abode;
May we also pass beyond the gates of life,
    welcomed by you, O Father, and your Son.

Peter of Alexandria

(died 311)

In 300, a man named Peter was made bishop of the Egyptian city of Alexandria. When the Christians began to be persecuted in the city, around the year 306, Peter fled. When he returned, he was arrested by the Roman officials under the general orders of Emperor Maximin. He was forced into slave labor for the Romans and then beheaded on November 25, 311. This prayer, in which Peter prays to be the "seal of the persecution," proved prophetic, for he was indeed one of the last Christians to be martyred by the Romans during that time, and the history books refer to him as "the seal and completion" of the Diocletian martyrs.

Silence the Storm

Jesus Christ, Son and Word of God,
> hear me, your suppliant.
Silence the storm that rises against
> your church;
Let the pouring out of my blood,
> as your servant,
be a seal of the persecution
> of your flock.

Lucian of Antioch

(died 312)

Lucian was a popular priest and writer in the ancient city of Antioch. As a leading scholar and theologian, he attended some of the best universities and was praised by some of the era's most famous Christian thinkers. Though he wrote many books about the Bible and church doctrine, little has survived. But fame and success do not mean freedom from hardship, and his faith was put to the test in 303, when he was arrested. For nine years he survived torture and the privation of prison. In 312, after a final chance to reject his faith, he delivered a famous speech in which he declared his willingness to be a martyr rather than reject God. He was executed shortly after that. Of all his writings, this speech is almost the only thing to have survived, though one can't help feeling that Lucian would have preferred it that way. Here is that famous prayer:

The Honor of Your Name

We offer you our simple praise, Lord Jesus,
    for, unworthy as we are,
You have defended us from the errors of the pagans,
    and in your mercy;
You have allowed us to come to this time of suffering
    for the honor of your name.
As you have permitted us to share in the glory
    of your saints.
We offer you glory and praise
    and we commend to your keeping our lives and our souls.

The Last Martyrs
of Rome

Although the details are sketchy, Theodota is believed to have been a prostitute in the city of Philippopolis, in Thrace (southeastern Balkans), who gave up her profession when she became a Christian. But a greater sacrifice awaited her. In 318, when the local prefect ordered all the citizens of the region—both Christian and non-Christian—to take part in the festival of the Roman god Apollo, Theodota was one of the first to refuse publicly. Her example gave hundreds of other Christians the courage to do the same, and soon Theodota was arrested as the ring-leader of the protest. She was cruelly tortured and finally stoned to death. This prayer is believed to have been spoken by her before her death. Notice that she refers to Rahab—a prostitute in the Old Testament—as someone to whom God had shown special mercy.

The Greater Crown

I worship you, O Christ,
    and I thank you that I have been
    counted worthy to suffer for your name.
Let me grasp the greater crown.
As you showed mercy to Rahab,
    and received the penitent thief,
    turn not your mercy from me.

Jonas of Beth-Iasa

(died 327)

After the time of Diocletian, the most violent persecutions of Christians took place in Persia, even after the Roman Empire had become officially Christian. The ruler of Persia, Shapur II, was a powerful enemy of the Christian Roman emperor, Constantius II. In spite of imperial edicts to the contrary, Shapur, as shah of his country, continued to persecute Christians, including two brothers, Jonas and Barachisius, who were from the town of Beth-Iasa. The brothers believed it was their Christian duty to comfort those in prison who were being tortured and facing execution. This led to their own arrest. An eyewitness account states they were ordered to worship the sun, moon, fire, and water. They refused. Jonas was then tortured and thrown into a frozen pond to die. When it was discovered that he had, in fact, survived, his body was placed in a wine press and he was crushed to death. Awaiting death, he spoke this prayer:

Seed Sown

Our life is seed,
> sown in the earth to rise again
> in the world to come,
Where we will be renewed by Christ
> in immortal life.
I did not frame this body,
> nor will I destroy it;
God, you gave me life,
> you will also restore it.

Simeon of Seleucia

(died about 339)

Shah Shapur II also accused a man named Simeon, the bishop of Seleucia, of treason for communicating with the shah's enemy, Emperor Constantius II. Simeon was therefore ordered to convert to Zoroastrianism, the official religion of Persia, and to worship the sun god alone. When Simeon refused, declaring, "The sun itself went into mourning when its Creator and Master died on the cross," the king had him tortured and imprisoned. On Good Friday, about the year 339, Bishop Simeon was forced to watch a hundred people from his church beheaded. Then he himself was executed in the same manner. In the following prayers, Simeon prays for an end to such cruel persecutions and then for the salvation of those who were to kill him.

The Crown of the Martyr

Lord, grant me this crown for which I have longed;
    for I have loved you with all my heart and all my soul.
I long to see you, to be filled with joy, and to find rest.
Then I will no longer have to witness the suffering of my congregation,
    the destruction of your churches, the overthrow of your altars,
    the persecution of your priests, the abuse of the defenseless,
    the departure from truth, and the large flock
    I watched over diminished by this time of trial.

I no longer wish to see those I considered my friends change
within their hearts, becoming angry and seeking my death;
or have those who are my true friends taken from me
by this persecution, while their killers order us about.
Even so, I intend to endure and show my vocation openly
in the course that is set before me,
so that I may be an example to all.
I have had the place of honor at the table;
I shall also have the place of precedence when it comes
to dying—
I will be the first to offer my blood.
I will then enter with my brothers into that life
which knows no troubles, no cares, no worries;
a life in which there will be neither persecutors
nor persecuted, neither oppressor nor oppressed,
neither tyrants nor victims.
In that life I will find neither the threats of kings
nor the insult of prefects;
no tribunal will judge me or cause me to fear,
no violence or coercion will be found.
Once I have set my steps in your way, I will stumble no more.
There, my weary body will find healing and rest,
for the Anointed One will be the oil placed upon us.
My heart's anguish will fade when I partake of you,
the Chalice of our salvation.
My Joy and my Consolation,
you will wipe away the tears from my eyes.

Lord Jesus, you prayed for those who placed you upon the cross
    and told us to pray for our enemies.
Stephen, your deacon, prayed for those who put him to death
    and you received his spirit.
Receive the souls of my brothers
    and receive my spirit with theirs.
Set us among the martyrs who have come before us
    and have received the crown of victory;
Set us among the holy apostles and blessed prophets.
Lord, bring to faith those who persecute us and put us to death,
    and do not count this against them as sin.
May they come to the knowledge that you are God.
Lord, bless all those in this land
    who you entrusted to my care.
Protect all the faithful as the apple of your eye.
In the midst of all these troubles,
    may they find shelter under the shadow of your wings.
Stay with them until the end of the age, as you promised.
Lord, bless this city that has witnessed our capture
    and our crowning.
I pray that your cross may keep it true to the faith
    now and forever.

                                        Amen.

Gustazad of Seleucia

(died about 339)

A man named Gustazad lived in Seleucia, Persia, and he was among the hundred believers who were martyred along with their local bishop, Simeon (see previous reading). This was around the year 339, during the persecutions instigated by Shapur II. Early sources say that Gustazad spoke the following prayer before his death.

A Lost Sheep

Lord Jesus, I give you praise:
I was a lost sheep, and you brought me back;
I strayed from your flock,
    but your shepherd came and found me.
He sought me out and brought me back to be offered
    with those sheep prepared for sacrifice.
I was returned to be a child of the apostles,
    a brother to those in the west
    who had received the crown,
    and an example to your people in the east.
Keep them all, do not let them lose the true faith.
Father, Son, and Holy Spirit, true God, Glorious King,
    whom all that worship the Holy Trinity,
    in heaven and on earth,
    will ever confess, ages without end.

                Amen.

Sadoth of Seleucia

(died about 340)

After Simeon's death, a man named Sadoth became the new bishop of Seleucia. For fear of Shapur II, Sadoth and the members of his church went into hiding. During that time, Sadoth had a vision of his impending martyrdom, and his description of that vision is the first reading given below, "The Ladder." The vision proved prophetic, for Sadoth and 128 people from his church were eventually arrested by Shapur's soldiers and brought before the king. When Shapur asked Sadoth whether he would rather worship the Persian sun god or die, Sadoth replied, "I shall not die." His full response is the second reading shown below. Sadoth and all 128 members of his church were executed.

The Ladder

A ladder was set before me in my sleep,
    surrounded by light,
    stretching from earth to heaven.
My friend Simeon was seated at the top, in great glory,
    and when he saw me at the bottom, smiling, he said,
"Climb up, Sadoth, do not fear.
    I climbed up yesterday; it is your turn today."
He meant that after his death last year,
    I am to follow him.

I Shall Not Die

I shall not die,
    but live and reign
eternally with God,
    and with Jesus Christ his Son.
So kill us as soon as you please—
    still, we will not worship the sun.

Sabas the Goth

(died about 372)

As a young man, Sabas, who lived in the Gothic area of what is today known as Romania, became a Christian and began to serve the church in the city of Targoviste. Although he survived several waves of persecution, Sabas was eventually arrested by a group of soldiers and ordered to eat meat that had been sacrificed to the pagan gods of the Goths. He refused and was repeatedly tortured along with about fifty other believers. Finally, he was thrown into the Mussovo River and drowned. His final words were:

On the Other Side

Blessed are you, Lord,
    and may your Son's name
    be blessed forevermore.
I can see what those who
    persecute me cannot;
On the other side of this river
    there is a multitude
Waiting to receive my soul
    and carry it to glory.

ntercisus is not the last name of the man named James, who was martyred during the second great persecution of Christians in Persia, around the year 421. *Intercisus* means "cut to pieces," which is exactly how this martyr died. Although different, conflicting accounts of this saint exist, the basic story is the same. As a fairly young man, James held a minor office in the court of Shah Bahram of Persia. His secret Christian faith, however, was discovered. In some versions, when he was asked to deny his faith, he stated, "I would rather be cut to pieces," while in other versions, this cruel torture was devised by one of the king's advisers. In any case, while awaiting execution, he spoke the following prayer.

A Branch of the Tree

This death, which seems too terrible,
    is little enough to gain eternal life.
Savior, receive a branch of the tree;
    it will decay but will flower again
    and be clothed with glory.
The vine dies in winter yet revives in spring.
Shall not this life that is cut down rise again?
My heart rejoices in the Lord,
    and my soul has exulted in your salvation.

Martin, Bishop of Rome

(died 655)

After becoming Bishop of Rome in 649, Martin became involved in an effort to suppress a growing heresy in the church (the belief that Jesus had no human will). He convened a council to deal with the matter but enraged Emperor Constans II in far-off Constantinople, who actually favored those who supported the heresy. The emperor contrived to have Martin arrested, brought to Constantinople to be jailed, beaten, and then sent into exile. In a letter to the church in Rome, Martin summarized the harsh treatment he received: "For forty-seven days, I have had no water to wash with. I am freezing and growing thin with dysentery. My food makes me vomit. But God sees all things, and I trust him." He probably died soon after of starvation, and he is considered the last Bishop of Rome to have been martyred. In the same letter, written during his exile, he wrote the following prayer:

He Is Present

I pray God that the Church may be preserved
    unmovable and steadfast in the true faith.
As to this wretched body, God will have care of it.
He is present and at hand; why should I be distressed?
I hope in his mercy that he will not prolong my course.

Martyrs of the Wars of Religion

Boris of Kiev

(died 1015)

Boris was the son of Vladimir, the first Christian prince of Russia. His father intended for Boris, his brother Gleb, and their half-brother, Svyatopolk, to rule Russia, each administering one-third of the country. But Svyatopolk, an enemy of Christianity who wished to rule Russia alone, secretly plotted his half-brothers' deaths. When a group of soldiers offered to protect Boris, he refused, stating that he would not use violence against his own brother. Instead, he prayed all night by the Alta River, but in the morning, Svyatopolk's assassins found Boris, attacked him with spears, and seized him just as Boris finished praying the prayer shown below. On the road to Kiev with Boris's seemingly dead body, the attackers discovered that he was still alive, and they finished the job with their swords. His brother Gleb was killed soon after.

Not from My Enemies

Lord Jesus Christ,
     who came to this world as a man
and suffered your passion,
     allowing your hands to be nailed to the cross
     for our sins,
give me the strength to endure my passion.
It comes not from my enemies,
     but from my own brother:
Yet, Lord, do not account it to him as sin.

Thomas à Becket
(1118–70)

After becoming Archbishop of Canterbury in 1162, Thomas à Becket found himself in a bitter dispute with the king of England, Henry II, over the issue of government control of the church. The conflict became so heated that one day the king casually mentioned to four knights that he wished he could be rid of Becket. Whether this was an order or simply a careless remark is not clear. Most likely, Henry was being intentionally vague, hoping that the knights would take the hint and that his own conscience, thereby, would be clear. The knights, however, took it as a direct command. They made their way to Canterbury Cathedral on December 29, 1170, and on the altar of his own church, they stabbed Becket, who spoke the following prayer before dying. The king's conscience was not clear, however, for the murder so shocked Europe that Henry was forced to perform public acts of penance the following year.

Into Your Hands

Into your hands, O Lord,
    I commend my spirit.
For the name of Jesus,
    and in defense of the Church,
I am willing to die.

Thomas More

(1478–1535)

Statesman and author Thomas More was Lord chancellor of England under King Henry VIII. His most famous book, *Utopia,* is one of the classics of English literature (it is the book in which More first coined the word *utopia*—an imaginary land of social perfection). More resigned from office after refusing to sign an oath stating that only the king—not the pope—had authority over the English church. For his refusal to side with Henry in his disputes with the Church of Rome, More was eventually charged with high treason and imprisoned. One of the main issues was More's refusal to acknowledge Henry's divorce of his wife, Catherine of Aragon—divorce, apart from a papal decree, being considered illegal at the time. More was imprisoned in the Tower of London in 1532 and finally beheaded three years later, on July 6, 1535. He wrote this prayer during his imprisonment.

In All My Fear

Good Lord, give me the grace,
    in all my fear and agony,
To have recourse to that great fear
    and wonderful agony that you, my Savior,
Had at the Mount of Olives before your
    most bitter passion;
And in meditating thereon,
    to conceive spiritual comfort
    and consolation profitable for my soul.

William Laud
(1573–1645)

F aith and politics have always been hot topics. In the seventeenth century, William Laud, the Archbishop of Canterbury, was one of the most influential Christians during an especially troubled time in England's history. Under King Charles I, Laud aggressively worked to counter the influence of the Calvinists, Puritans, and Presbyterians, in favor of maintaining the High Church doctrines of Anglicanism. He was involved in many political and religious controversies. Although his edicts were often heavy-handed, he believed they were what the times demanded, and the sincerity of his faith is beyond doubt.

Eventually, he provoked riots in Scotland by insisting that Scottish churches adopt the Anglican *Book of Common Prayer*. As the unrest grew, developing into what was called "the Bishops' War," the English Parliament decided to root out the problem at its source. To pacify the rebels, Parliament accused Laud of high treason, even though no specific evidence of wrongdoing was presented. Laud was arrested in 1641 and spent the next four years locked in the Tower of London, where he was finally beheaded on January 10, 1645. Just before his death, he spoke this moving prayer from the execution platform.

Lord, I am coming as fast as I can;
I know I must pass through the shadow of death
    before I can come to you,
But it is only the mere shadow of death,
    a little darkness upon nature:
But you, by your merits and passion,
    have broken through the jaws of death.
The Lord receive my soul, and have mercy on me,
    and bless this kingdom with peace and plenty,
    and with brotherly love and charity,
that there may not be this effusion of Christian
    blood among them,
for Jesus Christ's sake, if it be your will.
Lord, receive my soul.

Charles Stuart

harles I was king of Great Britain and Ireland from 1625 until his death—a time marked by some of the most violent upheavals on English soil, culminating in the English Civil War. England's Parliament was then asserting more power, and Charles hotly resisted their growing independence. Eventually, by an order of Parliament, Charles was arrested, tried by a court of sixty-seven judges, and executed on January 30, 1649, as a tyrant and enemy of the nation. Though considered a weak king who brought many of his disasters upon himself, he is listed among the martyrs because his death stemmed in part from his determination to defend the Church of England. In the end, he met his death bravely and with great faith, as can be seen by his final words:

An Incorruptible Crown

I go from a corruptible
    to an incorruptible crown;
Where no disturbance can be,
    no disturbance at all.

The Missionary Martyrs

Francis de Capillas
(1608–48)

Francis Ferdinand de Capillas was born in Spain in 1608. He entered a Dominican monastery at the age of seventeen, and at twenty-three, he volunteered as a missionary to the Philippines. In spite of hardships in the disease-infested jungles, he longed for greater challenges and asked to be transferred to a more dangerous mission field. Hoping to be sent to Japan, where many missionaries had died, he was sent instead to Fukien, China. After several years, the region was invaded by Tartars, and Francis was taken prisoner. At his trial, he was accused of witchcraft, spying, and refusing to "sacrifice to the ancestors." Despite suffering many tortures in prison, he managed to convert the jailer and several prisoners to Christianity. At last, in 1648, the judges, baffled by Francis's obstinate faith, condemned him to beheading on the false charge that he was in league with the rebel army then besieging the city. Declaring his willingness to die for Jesus, he wrote the following prayer.

No Other Object

I have no home but the world,
    no bed but the ground,
no food but what Providence sends me
    from day to day,
and no other object but to do your will
    and suffer, if need be,
for the glory of Jesus Christ
and for the eternal happiness
    of those who believe in his name.

John Ri

(died 1839)

The history of Christian missions in Korea began with much bloodshed. Since the eighteenth century, several waves of persecution swept the country, culminating in 1866, when more than eight thousand Korean Christians were executed for their faith. In one of the earlier waves, in 1838, a Korean Catholic man named John Ri, as well as more than two hundred others, died when the authorities in Korea felt that Christianity had become too popular among the people. John Ri was working as an associate of the Paris Foreign Missions at the time. The following prayer was written by John Ri as he awaited execution.

I Cannot Repay Such Mercy

The sins of my entire life,
    by which I have so often offended you,
my God, weigh me down
    like a mountain of my own making.
I wonder, "What will be the end
    of all this?"
Yet, I do not lose hope.
I cannot bear this alone;
    I know I am weak.

But your strength will keep
    me from falling.
The prayers of others will
    uphold me in my time of need.
I cannot repay such mercy;
    to offer my life is only right.

rench missionary priest Théophane Vénard, born in 1829, was only twenty-three years old when he sailed for China. After serving in Hong Kong for several years, he went to Western Tonkin to minister to nearly ten thousand Chinese Christians who were suffering severe persecution. Théophane was respected even by many of his persecutors for his patient love and gentility. After five years of hiding in caves and preaching secretly at night—and sometimes in broad daylight—he was arrested and imprisoned in a cage, which was suspended in the open air. During that time, he wrote many endearing letters of consolation to his family in France, especially to his brother, Eusebius, and sister, Melanie, for whom he had a special affection. He was finally beheaded on February 2, 1861. The following words are extracts from those letters.

All My Earthly Happiness

I know the sorrow I will bring to my family.
It has cost me tears of blood to take such a step
    and give those I love such pain.
Who is there who cared for home
    and family more than I?

All my earthly happiness was to be found there,
But you, O God, who united us with such
    tender affection,
weaned me from what I love that
    I might serve you.

Undreamed-of Harmonies

I do not regret this world;
    my soul thirsts for the waters of eternal life.
My exile is over.
I am approaching the soil of my true country;
    earth vanishes, heaven opens, I go to God. . . .
About two feet from my cage,
    a feeble oil lamp throws a wavering glimmer
    on this sheet of Chinese paper
    and enables me to trace these few lines.
From day to day, I expect my sentence—perhaps tomorrow. . . .
Within a few hours my soul shall quit this earth,
    exile over and battle won.
I shall mount upward and enter into our true home.
There, among God's elect,
    I shall gaze upon what the eye of man cannot imagine,
    hear undreamed-of harmonies,
    enjoy a happiness
    that the heart cannot remotely comprehend.

Modern Martyrs

Noel Pinot
(1747–94)

father Noel Pinot, a Catholic priest in the French parish of Louroux Béconnais, lived near Paris at the time of the French Revolution. When the revolutionary government ordered him to take an oath recognizing their authority over the clergy, he refused. Though he was stripped of his priesthood as a result, he continued to conduct secret services for his parishioners. Eventually, he was arrested while conducting a Communion service, and he was escorted to prison. Twelve days later, on February 21, 1794, still wearing his priest's robes, he was taken to the guillotine for execution. Before mounting the platform, he was overheard to recite the following prayer, a paraphrase of Psalm 43, which is a psalm usually recited by a priest at the altar of a church.

I Will Approach the Altar of God

I will enter unto the altar of God,
   to God who gives the joy of my youth.
Give judgment to me, O God,
   and defend my cause against the ungodly:
Deliver me from the wicked and deceitful person.
   For you are the God of my strength.
Send out your light and your truth,
   that they may lead me:
And bring me to your holy hill,
   to the place where you dwell.
I will enter unto the altar of God,
   to God who gives the joy of my youth.

Gabra Michael

(1788–1855)

Gabra Michael, who was born in Ethiopia, became a Christian in 1844 and joined the Roman Catholic Church. He was ordained as a priest in 1851. At that time in Ethiopia, however, Theodore II, the emperor of the country, was actively persecuting Catholics and ordered that Michael and four of his companions be arrested. After being dragged in his chains through the streets, Gabra later died from neglect and abuse on August 28, 1855. He spoke these words while in prison:

If I Live . . .

Let me be steadfast in my faith
    to the end.
I have no hope of seeing my brethren
    again in this life.
If they kill me, let me die
    as a witness to my faith;
If I live, let me go on
    proclaiming it.

Michael Pro

What country in the Western Hemisphere has a more noble Catholic history than Mexico? And yet, after the revolution of 1924, religious orders were banned by law. Michael Pro (whose full name was Michael Augustine Pro-Juarez) was a Jesuit priest who had been politically active in the Young Christian Workers movement. After performing his religious duties in secret for a time, he was arrested on trumped-up charges. On November 23, 1927, he was executed by a government firing squad. Before he died, he pronounced this blessing on his persecutors:

Viva Cristo Rey! (Hail Christ Our King!)

May God have mercy on you!
May God bless you!
Lord, you know that I am innocent.
I forgive my enemies with all my heart.
Hail, Christ, our King.

An Anonymous Child Martyr
(died around 1943)

Who wrote the following prayer? No one knows. It was scrawled on a scrap of paper and placed inside the clothing of a child who was killed at Ravensbruck, a concentration camp where the Nazis killed thousands upon thousands of innocent people. Whoever wrote the prayer may have died in the same gas chambers as the child.

Remember

O Lord, remember not only the men and women of good will,
    but also those of ill will.
But, do not remember all of the suffering
    they have inflicted upon us:
Instead remember the fruits we have borne
    because of this suffering—
our fellowship, our loyalty to one another, our humility,
    our courage, our generosity,
the greatness of heart that has grown from this trouble.
When our persecutors come to be judged by you,
    let all of these fruits that we have borne
    be their forgiveness.

Dietrich Bonhoeffer

(1906-45)

One of the most difficult questions of the twentieth century was: How could such a vast majority of German Christians turn a blind eye to the atrocities committed by Adolf Hitler and the Nazis? How was it possible for so many to say so little?

Some Christians did speak up, however, and many of them died. Best known among them was Lutheran pastor Dietrich Bonhoeffer, who wrote several books of theology, including *The Cost of Discipleship,* a provocative title, considering the price he himself was to pay for his discipleship. Aware of Hitler's policy toward the Jews, Bonhoeffer knew that all moral people everywhere should commit themselves to stopping the Nazi regime. So he decided to take part in a conspiracy to assassinate Hitler. In his own mind Bonhoeffer weighed the personal evil of murder against the evil of Hitler's murder of literally millions of people, and for Bonhoeffer, the answer was inescapable. But the plot was uncovered, Bonhoeffer was arrested, and he was executed only days before the war ended. The following prayer was written by Pastor Bonhoeffer in his cell as he awaited his execution by hanging.

Help Me to Pray

O God, early in the morning I cry to you.
Help me to pray,
    and to concentrate my thoughts on you:

I cannot do this alone.
In me there is darkness,
    but with you there is light;
I am lonely;
    but you do not leave me;
I am feeble in heart,
    but with you there is help;
I am restless,
    but with you there is peace.
In me there is bitterness,
    but with you there is patience;
I do not understand your ways,
    but you know the way for me ...
Restore me to liberty,
And enable me so to live now
    that I may answer before you and before me.
Lord, whatever this day may bring,
Your name be praised.

The following are Bonhoeffer's final words, which beautifully express the certainty of his faith.

The Beginning

This is the end
    but for me
It is the beginning
    of life.

Yona Kanamuzeyi

(about 1918 – 1964)

ather Yona Kanamuzeyi was an Anglican priest in Rwanda, then in the throes of a civil war between the Tutsi and the Hutu tribes. As a respected clergyman and prominent Tutsi, Father Kanamuzeyi's influence was enormous—so much so that he was feared by the Hutu. Kanamuzeyi labored untiringly in a Tutsi refugee camp, ministering to more than six thousand believers through the work of his central church and the many village churches he helped to establish. In January 1964, Hutu troops arrested Kanamuzeyi and his friend Andrew Kayumba. They were driven to a Hutu camp, where the officer in charge ordered them to pray. Knowing what was coming, Kanamuzeyi asked God to accept his life as a sacrifice and to forgive the soldiers who would kill him. The priest was then marched to a bridge, shot, and his body thrown into the stream. His friend, later released, told the story to the church—and the world— thereby preserving the memory of one of modern Africa's great Christian martyrs. The following prayer was spoken by Father Kanamuzeyi while serving in the refugee camp.

You Know All About Me

O God, it was you who called me
    and sent me to this place.
You know all about me—
    the days I have lived
    and the days that are let to me.
If it is your will to call me home,
    I leave the decision to you.

Oscar Romero

(1917 – 80)

In the 1970s and '80s, El Salvador was under the heel of a military dictatorship, and, as is common in such cases, the country's poor suffered most. Fortunately, they had a champion in Oscar Romero, the Archbishop of San Salvador. He worked to defend the rights of the poor, oppose the government's unjust policies, and encourage the church to extend its work into every area of society.

In March of 1980, an abandoned attaché case was found near the altar of Romero's church. It contained a bomb—that failed to go off. After that, he insisted on traveling and working alone so as not to expose others to danger. While the archbishop was celebrating Communion two weeks later, on March 24, 1980, a red four-door Volkswagen drove past the front doors of the church. A professional assassin from a right-wing military death squad was in the passenger seat. The single bullet fired from the car found its target and killed Oscar Romero. In the weeks before his death, Romero uttered these thoughts about martyrdom:

God's Church . . . Will Never Perish

Martyrdom is a grace of God that
    I do not believe I deserve.
But if God accepts the sacrifice of my life,
    let my blood be a seed of freedom
and the sign that hope will soon be reality.
    Let my death, if it is accepted by God,
be for my people's freedom and a witness of hope.

You may say, if they succeed in killing me,
  that I pardon and bless those who do it.
Would, indeed, they might be convinced not
  to waste their time.
A bishop will die, but God's Church,
  which is the people, will never perish.

Bahram Dehqani-Tafti of Iran

(died 1981)

The following prayer was not written by the martyred believer but by his father. Bahram Dehqani-Tafti was the son of the bishop of the Episcopal Church in Iran, Hassan Dehqani-Tafti. As the Islamic revolution took hold of the country, the family was forced to flee, but on May 6, 1980, before they could escape to Lebanon, Bahram, who was known as a Christian, was stopped by members of the Revolutionary Guard, dragged from his car, and shot to death. In response to his son's death, his father, Hassan, wrote this prayer.

A Father's Prayer Upon the Murder of His Son

O God,
We remember not only our son but also his murderers;
Not because they killed him in the prime of his youth
    and made our hearts bleed and our tears flow;
Not because with this savage act
    they have brought further disgrace on the name of our country
    among the civilized nations of the world;
But because through their crime we now follow
    your footsteps more closely in the way of sacrifice.

The terrible fire of this calamity burns up
    all selfishness and possessiveness in us;
Its flame reveals the depth of depravity and meanness
            and suspicion,
    the dimension of hatred
    and the measure of sinfulness in human nature;
It makes obvious as never before our need to trust in God's love
    as shown in the cross of Jesus and his resurrection;
Love that make us free from hate toward our persecutors;
Love that brings patience, forbearance, courage,
    loyalty, humility, generosity, greatness of heart;
Love that more than ever deepens our trust
    in God's final victory
    and his eternal designs for the Church and for the world;
Love that teaches us how to prepare ourselves
    to face our own day of death.
O God,
Our son Bahram's blood has multiplied the fruit of the Spirit
    in the soil of our souls;
So when his murderers stand before you on the day of judgment,
Remember the fruit of the Spirit
    by which they have enriched our lives.
And forgive.

Afterword
by Madeleine L'Engle

The prayers that Duane Arnold has gathered together are a beautiful compilation of the love of Christian martyrs for their God and the Lord Jesus Christ. This is a book to be sipped, and turned to again and again.

The love of the martyrs is in marked contrast to the fear and hate of those who made martyrs. The words of Shenoufe the Copt in his blessing of Jesus are an affirmation of the love of God that is with us always, in weal and woe. Theodota of Philippopolis gives thanks that she has been counted worthy to suffer in Christ's name, and urges, "As you showed mercy to Rahab, and received the penitent thief, turn not your mercy from me." ...

What has caused people throughout the centuries to want to kill other people for bringing them good news? Surely the news that the first Christian martyrs brought to the world was extraordinarily good: "God so loved the world that he gave his only begotten Son, that whosoever believes in him should not perish, but have everlasting life. For God sent not his Son into the world to condemn the world; but that the world through him might be saved." What could be more wonderful! Yet the news of God's love has always frightened those who believe only in God's wrath.

It is ironic that many of the heresies for which Christians have been burned, stoned, and thrown to wild beasts have been (and still are) heresies of love. It was once a heresy to believe that God in his infinite love surely would *not* condemn unbaptized infants to the flames of hell—surely a heresy of love. Montanus affirms that "we all have the same spirit, and this is what unites us in our actions and all that we do together.... To be your children, we must love one another." Another heresy of love.

The martyrs of our time may well also affirm heresies of love, and their persecutors may not be people who do not believe in Christ as Lord, but those who call themselves Christians. There is a sad tendency today for Christians to seek to condemn other Christians and to read books not looking for love and courage, or with any regard for content, but looking for ugliness and for Satan. We do tend to find what we look for. If we look for Satan we will find Satan, and that is dangerous indeed. As Christians, we must look for Christ, and for love. Nemesian of Numidia cries out, "Let us help each other by our prayers, so that God and Christ and the whole choir of angels may come to our aid in our time of suffering, when we shall need their assistance the most."

Indeed we need to help each other in this new century. We know far more about the nature of God's universe than we did a century ago, and this knowledge of the wonders of God's glory is frightening to some people who want to hang on to the old human-centered way of looking at what God has made. There is a new and troublesome fear of the imagination—though without it, how can anyone believe in the Incarnation, the Power that created all of the galaxies willingly limiting itself to be one of us for love of us! And this fear is expressing itself in a new kind of book burning and witch-hunting.

Jesus called us to be loving, to be vulnerable, to be as little children, and it is a calling too frightening for those who insist on living with certainty. The martyrs through the ages have known terrible uncertainty redeemed by that perfect love that casts out fear. Clement of Rome speaks deeply to my heart when he says, "Almighty God, Father of our Lord Jesus Christ, grant, we pray, that we might be grounded and settled in your truth by the coming of your Holy Spirit into our hearts. What we do not know, reveal to us; what is lacking within us, make complete; that which we do know, confirm in us; and keep us blameless in your service, through Jesus Christ our Lord."

The loving hearts of many martyrs causes them to pray for those who persecute them, as Jesus taught us that we should. Thelica of Abitine pleads, "O God most high, do not consider the actions of my persecutors as sin. God, have pity on them." Perhaps the most heartrending of all such prayers is one found in the clothing of a dead child at Ravensbruck concentration camp, which begins, "O Lord, remember not only the men and women of good will, but also those of ill will," and ends, "When our persecutors come to be judged by you, let all of these fruits that we have borne be their forgiveness."

And Archbishop Oscar Romero writes of his persecutors, "You may say, if they succeed in killing me, that I pardon and bless those who do it. . . . A bishop will die, but God's Church, which is the people, will never perish." And Anglican Bishop Hassan Dehqani-Tafti almost echoes the child at Ravensbruck, "O God, our son Bahram's blood has multiplied the fruit of the Spirit in the soil of our souls; so when his murderers stand before you on the day of judgment, remember the fruit of the Spirit by which they have enriched our lives. And forgive."

Forgive. Love. Seek for the Truth that will give us life and life more abundantly. Trust in the message that these prayers leave with us, a message crucial for our time.

Madeleine L'Engle
from the foreword
to the original edition
of this book,
Prayers of the Martyrs

The Voice of the Martyrs . . .
Serving the persecuted church since 1967

The Voice of the Martyrs is a nonprofit, interdenominational organization dedicated to assisting the persecuted church worldwide. VOM was founded over thirty years ago by Pastor Richard Wurmbrand, who was imprisoned in Communist Romania for fourteen years for his faith in Jesus Christ. His wife, Sabina, was imprisoned for three years. In the 1960s Richard, Sabina, and their son, Mihai, were ransomed out of Romania and came to the United States. Through their travels, the Wurmbrands spread the message of the atrocities that Christians face in restricted nations, while establishing a network of offices dedicated to assisting the persecuted church. The Voice of the Martyrs continues in this mission around the world today through five main purposes.

- To encourage and empower Christians to fulfill the Great Commission in areas of the world where they are persecuted for their involvement in propagating the gospel of Jesus Christ. We accomplish this by providing Bibles, literature, radio broadcasts, and other forms of aid.

- To give relief to the families of Christian martyrs in these areas of the world.
- To equip local Christians to win to Christ those persecutors who are opposed to the gospel in countries where believers are actively persecuted for their Christian witness.
- To undertake projects of encouragement, helping believers rebuild their lives and Christian witness in countries that have formerly suffered Communist oppression.
- To emphasize the fellowship of all believers by informing the world of atrocities committed against Christians and by remembering their courage and faith.

The Voice of the Martyrs publishes a free monthly newsletter, giving updates on the persecuted church and suggesting ways you can help. To subscribe, call or write:

The Voice of the Martyrs
P.O. Box 443
Bartlesville, OK 74005
(800) 747-0085
e-mail address: thevoice@vom-usa.org
Web site: www.persecution.com